Sing Like the Whippoorwill

Sing Like the Whippoorwill

Fable by Stafford Betty

Illustrations by Sylvia Zimmerman

TWENTY-THIRD PUBLICATIONS

Mystic, Connecticut

Twenty-Third Publications
P.O. Box 180
Mystic, CT 06355
(203) 536-2611

Illustrations and cover design by Sylvia Zimmerman
Book designed by William Baker
Edited by John G. van Bemmel

ISBN 0-89622-324-8
Library of Congress Catalog Card Number 86-51539

Contents

THE EVIL

A mist that smelled of decaying leaves hung in the motionless air, and the teeming Kingdom rang with shrill birdsong from one end to the other. As the sun rose above the treetops, it wormed its way down through the haze and singed the forest floor with shafts of mote-filled light, while a faint new moon hung distantly and apprehensively in the pale blue sky. Soon the morning's first breath of air stirred, and the ferns that hugged the woodland ponds wagged unsuspectingly, while the ponds themselves began to flutter at their dark leeward edges.

Deep in the shadows of huge trees beside one pond in particular, an evil as black and thick and sticky as tar lay hidden. Equally hidden, hovering unseen over the forest, was a very different kind of being. His name would have seemed alien to a forest dweller, so we will call him simply the Guardian. For centuries he had watched

invisibly over the Kingdom of the Green Fern Forest—for this was his assignment—and in its own way it had flourished. But never had he been allowed to influence its destiny in a direct way. Never • until now.

Never before had the Guardian come down so low to earth. Four bugs in particular were the focus of his rapt attention. These four, out of millions and millions, he had carefully, agonizingly hand-picked. Now conditions were ideal, they were exactly right, the time—it seemed impossible!—had actually come. With a rapturous shudder he recalled the Great Parent's final command: "Never violate their natures, neither in their world nor in ours." As the last traces of mist fled before the incandescent glare of the sun, the Guardian surveyed the forest one last time, and his heart beat like a tight drum. All the study, all the preparation, all the waiting of centuries. Now at last.

There was Felicity the firefly in her usual place snug up against her stone at the edge of the pond. Earnest, cheerful, plain, artless Felicity: she was such a good girl. The night just ended had been an especially good one for her. She thought with delight of the way she and her firefly friends had lit up the deep black forest with their rhythmic prayers of green-gold light. How thrilling it had been! If only the other bugs of the Kingdom could understand, then they would glow too!

With these thoughts in mind she touched the medallion that she always wore round her neck, folded her antennae together, and asked the Great Parent to reveal his son—his only son, the Firefly Son—to all the other bugs of the Kingdom. Then she drew her home-ly head up under her orange hood and fell fast asleep, oblivious to the mortal danger that lurked in secret upland shadows not far from where she lay.

And there was Skeeter the water-skater meditating in his

usual place at the edge of the pond under the ferns—the same ferns that shaded the stone next to which Felicity slept. Skeeter the water-skater was by nature a high-strung, jumpy, fidgety bug—the last sort you might expect to meditate. Yet there he sat, his straggly black guru's beard dangling in the water between his skinny knock-knees. Balanced on his six stick-like feet which dimpled the water without breaking it, he tried to shut out the bright world of color and shape which he scornfully dismissed as an illusion. What a comical sight he seemed to most of his fellow insects! Yet he was unconcerned.

As he looked out across the pond—a flat white gleaming plain from where he stood—he congratulated himself that he was not a land-dweller. Then he closed his squinty eyes and tried to find the peaceful, joyful, summer-morning Self within—the one and only Reality. But he could not; he sensed instead—actually he was not

4

sure if he sensed it by the power of his yoga or merely imagined it—he sensed something so dark, malevolent, and odious that he shivered.

And there was Miller the millipede out for his morning walk, only a few yards away from the sun-dappled ferns under which Felicity the firefly slept and Skeeter the water-skater meditated. Miller the millipede was a rustic, a country boy, and he delighted in the feel of damp black earth under his seventy-four feet.

As he passed under a blade of prickly sedge that rubbed greenly up against his green-spotted black fenders, he reached back with one of his seven-jointed antennae and adjusted his backpack. "Good to be alive!" he said out loud in that drawl of his. He hadn't come across any of those fast-walking, self-important types who almost made him feel inferior.

He remembered with a sting some of the insults that the six-legged insects of the Kingdom threw at him—like "Joints," "Hose Head," and "Speedy"—but he forced himself not to care. Just nature,

nature green and giving, obedient and dependable, beautiful and almost shy—that's all he saw and heard and felt and smelled around him. Miller the millipede loved the way his long spongy body bent to the shapes and tingled to the textures of the green and the brown and the gray things he traversed. In seventy different ways, each unique, he felt one with the stick he was crossing as each foot, in succession, fell.

He knew nothing of the dark, evil plans being hatched unseen nearby, for he had no way of knowing anything—so he thought—unless it came through his senses. And his senses told him that it was a fine morning, a splendid morning for a hike.

Finally, there was Auntie the ant. Liberal-minded, ever curious, up on things, and full of advice (that's how she got her name), she was one of the leaders of her commune. On this particular day she had decided to strike out on her own in search of a new trail, a short cut, back to the nest.

As she veered off the old worn trail, her sister ants called out, "Be careful!" but Auntie only muttered "hmph!" Her six legs worked with machine-like precision, and her two antennae swept back and forth like radar. With her powerful pincers she balanced a portion of a thick green leaf over her head. Suddenly she found

herself alongside a pond she had
never seen before. The rotting
leaves of the forest floor made
progress difficult, and to make
matters worse her wire-rim glasses
kept clouding over. But she drove
on, for she was a leaf-cutter ant,
and leaf-cutter ants considered
themselves the proudest, bravest,
smartest, most enlightened insects
in the Kingdom.

 As she slogged through the nutbrown humus still wet with
dew, she began to feel dizzy, but she dismissed the dizziness as
unworthy of her. Just a little farther, she told herself, then she would
rest. And in fact she thought she saw something smooth and solid
in the shadows directly ahead. She boosted her leaf high above her
head and marched on. For all her brains, she hadn't an inkling of
the evil threat that the forest hid.

 The Guardian now hovered unseen just above the pond,
and the glowing aureole that surrounded him had turned from its
usual sunlight-white to a fiery pulsating orange. Seeing that the

meeting was imminent, he turned his penetrating gaze toward a thick clump of underbrush just inland from the pond. There it was waiting. Centuries had passed since the Guardian had been so close to such evil, and the shock of it felt like sand thrown in the face.

For an instant his aureole fluttered and dimmed, but then, his supernatural light again blazing forth, he gently and undetectably nudged the evil with his mighty intellect. The evil, though free to resist, greedily surrendered to its devouring habit, and turned in the direction of the stone by the pond.

THE AMBUSH

Like two moths drawn to flame from opposite directions, Miller the millipede and Auntie the leaf-cutter ant converged on the large stone under the ferns at the edge of the pond in the middle of the Green Fern Forest. Miller reached it first and started to crawl up. His feet felt the familiar wrinkles as they crossed the face of the stone, and this made him happy. Up, up he went—but what was that? He distinctly heard the pitter-patter of some insect's feet on the other side, and they seemed to be heading in his direction.

By now he had reached the ridge of the stone, and he peeped over. There, heading straight for him, was an ant balancing a leaf. Miller knew that ants could bite, so he lurched himself sideways in an effort to get out of the way. But he couldn't get the back half of himself out of the way in time. At the last instant he tried to shout, but his heart was already in his throat, and he couldn't

force the words out, no matter how hard he tried.

"Aaaaagh!" screamed the ant as she stumbled over Miller, her glasses flying in one direction and her leaf in another.

"What was that?" said Skeeter, suddenly roused from his meditation at the edge of the pond. As only a water-skater can, he jumped straight up out of the water, looking as if he had suffered a colossal hiccup. Then, as he settled back down, he noticed a piece of a thick green leaf tumbling down the face of the stone. It landed in the water near him, and floated.

Felicity the firefly had also heard the scream from her leafy bed. Just as she peeped up groggily, something came rattling down the face of the stone right at her.

"My glasses! My glasses!" screamed Auntie, who was

near-sighted.

Felicity's first instinct was not to get involved with strangers, but she remembered one of the teachings of the Firefly Son about loving one's enemy. "Here they are!" she sang out.

"Where—where are you?" cried out Auntie, into the great blurry world.

"I'll bring them up," said Felicity in her most cheerful, helpful voice. She buzzed her wings and flew up to the ridge of the stone with belly flashing and handed Auntie the glasses.

Auntie took them without so much as a thank you. All she

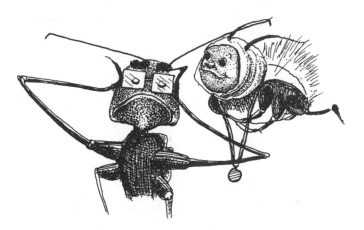

could think of was how to get away from such uncouth company. A lazy, worthless millipede was bad enough. But a firefly! Auntie had always detested them. She had never known one, but she regarded them all as floozies. The way they flashed their bellies about for all the world to see—it was obscene!

She was so anxious to get going that she considered leaving her leaf behind, but then she thought of her sisters back on the trail, all carrying their burdens back to the nest to farm.

"Did anyone see my leaf?" she said, trying to sound conciliatory.

No one as yet had noticed Skeeter. He was sitting quietly in the water near the base of the stone taking it all in, amused by this latest hubbub of land-dwellers. Now he wondered what on earth could be so important about the leaf floating at his side. The way those ants were always doing something, going somewhere, looking so serious. And the way they always stuck together—he had never seen an ant alone until now. Did they ever go off by themselves to think? Did they ever ask the ultimate questions? Skeeter doubted it. But if she simply had to have her leaf....

"Down here!" he called up. Then he pushed the leaf up to the edge of the stone and waited to see what would happen.

Auntie scrambled down the stone and lifted the leaf out of the water. She pretended not to notice the odd stick-like fellow from the watery world, and turned around to climb back up.

Skeeter was instantly incensed. He had deigned to help a land-dweller, and this was the result! "Don't you ants have any manners?" he sputtered in his strange jerky voice.

Auntie turned around and stared at the skater. His antennae twitched back and forth, up and down, in wide sweeps, as if he were fighting a two-handed duel with himself. Then he jumped straight up out of the water, his beard flying around like Spanish moss blowing in a gale. There was something comical but also very formidable about this weirdo, Auntie thought to herself.

"Thank you," she said, trying to sound sincere. Then she turned back around, lifted her burden high over her shoulders, and hurried up the stone.

Suddenly a faint current of air stealing out of the bowels

of the forest worked its way over the stone where Miller stood. He looked up at the canopy of giant ferns hanging over the stone, and he saw their ominous flutter. He sniffed again and again with his sensitive nose. And he felt that something was wrong. Dreadfully wrong.

"Smell that!" he said as he was preparing to leave, just as Auntie reached the top of the stone.

"Smell what?" she said with a trace of contempt in her raspy voice.

Nevertheless she froze. But all that she smelled was the rich dark duff of the forest floor, and that for most forest dwellers is like the smell of the air itself. She listened, but all she heard was the breeze slinking through the green cave of ferns shutting out the sun above. She looked around, but all she saw through her spectacles to alarm her was the fear in the millipede's wide-open eyes.

Then it happened. Out of a cover of dead leaves two huge figures loomed.

Auntie and Felicity scrambled down the rock in opposite directions as fast as they could go. But Miller was not equipped to run. So he just curled up on the stone in a little black-and-green ball and tried to be perfectly still. He watched in horror as the

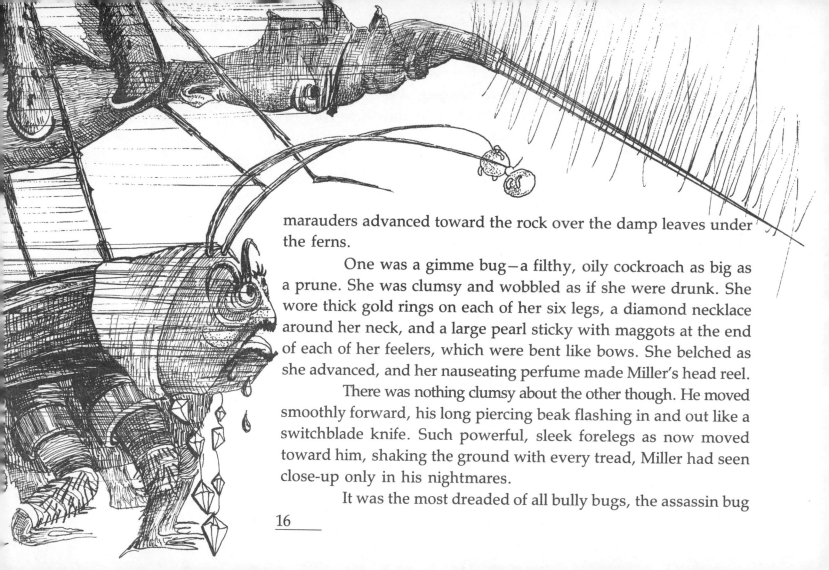

marauders advanced toward the rock over the damp leaves under the ferns.

One was a gimme bug—a filthy, oily cockroach as big as a prune. She was clumsy and wobbled as if she were drunk. She wore thick gold rings on each of her six legs, a diamond necklace around her neck, and a large pearl sticky with maggots at the end of each of her feelers, which were bent like bows. She belched as she advanced, and her nauseating perfume made Miller's head reel.

There was nothing clumsy about the other though. He moved smoothly forward, his long piercing beak flashing in and out like a switchblade knife. Such powerful, sleek forelegs as now moved toward him, shaking the ground with every tread, Miller had seen close-up only in his nightmares.

It was the most dreaded of all bully bugs, the assassin bug

with his cogwheel back, and Miller suddenly was sure that he was going to die. He already could feel the great beak plunging into his soft flesh just behind the head. He closed his eyes and waited in terror.

But at that moment something extraordinary happened. Like an eagle Felicity rose on her wings. With belly flashing, she dove at the advancing assassin. He swiped at her with one of his terrible red forelegs, but missed. Felicity circled back around and buzzed him again. She nipped one of his antennae as she passed.

Then all of a sudden Auntie rushed up to Miller from her hiding place behind a stick. "Get up! Get Up!" she shrieked. She flung her thick green leaf back into the pond, grabbed Miller by his backpack, and heaved him tumbling end over end down the face of the stone. Miller found himself in the water next to the leaf. "Get on!" she screamed.

Then there was a sound, a horrible, foul sound. "I want that light! Gimme that light! Kill her, you idiot! Do something!" The cockroach's booming voice reverberated through the forest like thunder. She wanted the light in the firefly's belly more than all her rings and jewels. And she craved wearing the firefly's orange hood as a hat. She would do anything to have these—anything. "Do something!" she shrieked.

But the assassin had met his match in Felicity. She kept flying in circles and buzzing him.

Then the greedy cockroach saw the millipede getting away. "The millipede!" she screamed. "I want that backpack! Gimme that backpack!"

The assassin bug looked at his girl friend and for an instant hated her. But then he smelled the intoxicating oils that she wore and saw her diamonds glitter. His muscles quivered, and he felt an insane rage sweep over him. He wanted a victim, any victim. His violent eyes riveted on the millipede dangling from a leaf at the edge of the water.

"Easy prey!" he grinned. And with his eyes blazing red and his fearsome dagger-beak lifted high, he charged like a fiend down the face of the stone.

18

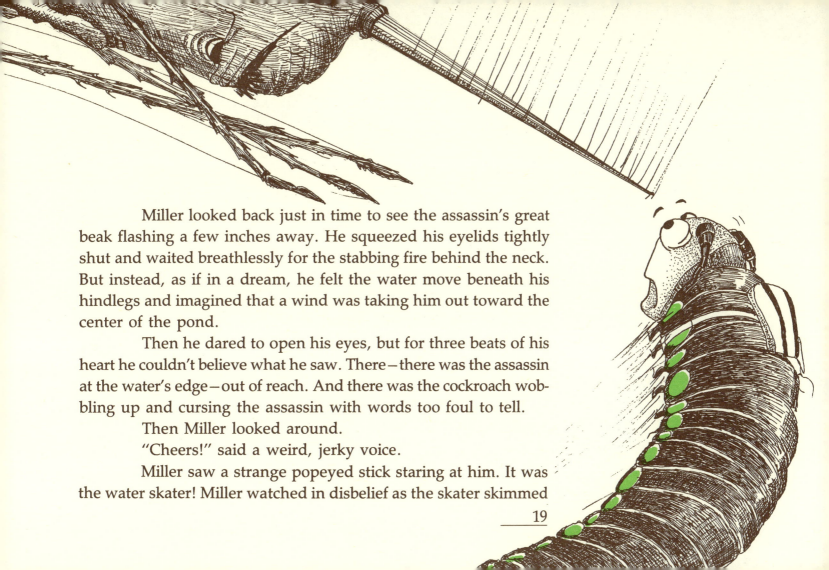

Miller looked back just in time to see the assassin's great beak flashing a few inches away. He squeezed his eyelids tightly shut and waited breathlessly for the stabbing fire behind the neck. But instead, as if in a dream, he felt the water move beneath his hindlegs and imagined that a wind was taking him out toward the center of the pond.

Then he dared to open his eyes, but for three beats of his heart he couldn't believe what he saw. There—there was the assassin at the water's edge—out of reach. And there was the cockroach wobbling up and cursing the assassin with words too foul to tell.

Then Miller looked around.

"Cheers!" said a weird, jerky voice.

Miller saw a strange popeyed stick staring at him. It was the water skater! Miller watched in disbelief as the skater skimmed

19

the pond's surface with sweeping oar-like strokes, pulling the leaf that the ant had carried along with him. The hot sun beat down on Miller's bruised black body, but he didn't even notice.

"Nothing to fear here," said the skater.

But Miller wasn't too sure. He half expected some malevolent trick at any moment. He wasn't about to let himself feel grateful. Not yet.

A little later the firefly flew over and sang out the all-clear. Skeeter pushed the leaf with Miller on it back toward shore.

20

THE JOURNEY

That night back in her nest after a delicious meal of choice fungus, Auntie couldn't sleep. She kept thinking about the millipede. She realized that she didn't even know his name, yet she had risked her life to save him. Why did she do such a foolish thing?

She thought of the way the four of them parted. They had gathered on the stone, but no one said anything. Yet she had wanted very much to say something. But what exactly was it? She had wanted to shout for joy, but she didn't. She had wanted to look into the eyes of the other three and smile, but when she looked at them she felt only shame, and she frowned instead. She hadn't wanted to leave the rock, but she forced herself to pick up her burden and head into the woods without so much as a goodbye. And now she couldn't sleep. She couldn't help feeling that there was some terribly important unfinished business that needed her immediate attention. Finally, she got up. She crawled up out of the nest and out into the night.

She started walking, walking alone, as ants seldom do. At first she didn't know where she was going. But gradually it dawned

on her that she was walking toward the stone. The stone beckoned, called out, and finally compelled. On and on she went. It grew light in the east, then bright crimson. Hurry, she thought. The stone, the stone. Then she found herself under the ferns next to the pond, and it was as if the sun had suddenly set. She stumbled over the dead leaves of the forest floor, but she did not slow her pace.

At last she saw the stone straight ahead, then felt its smooth surface under her sure feet. Up and up she climbed. And there, to her astonishment, were—the millipede, the skater, and the firefly! It was as if they had never left!

Each of them told a similar story. None could sleep, and each felt drawn back to the stone. Each was amazed by the power of the compulsion. None knew what to make of it. Worst of all, none knew now what to do.

Then transpired the strangest event in the history of the Kingdom. Out of the woods a bug unlike any ever seen glided toward the four. It did not quite walk and it did not quite fly. It was wingless, yet its feet did not touch the ground. It glowed, but not as the firefly from only one place in her body. It smiled, but not in a manner that any bug had ever smiled before. About all this the four later agreed.

But they did not agree about what kind of bug it was. The firefly was sure it was a firefly, but the ant was just as sure it was an ant. And where the skater saw six stick-like legs, the millipede saw seventy or more. But they all felt sure that it was this bug, whatever he or she was, that had called them back to the stone. And they all.heard him say the same thing:

"Do not be afraid, brothers and sisters. I am the Guardian of the Green Fern Forest. I have brought you together for a purpose that I cannot now reveal in full. Follow these instructions, and all will end well; this I promise. First, learn each other's names. Use them. Then go to the west. Go together. Keep your minds alert and your eyes wide open, and talk over what you learn along the way. Above all, search out what you have already learned, learned yesterday when you were first brought together on this stone, but do not yet know you have learned.

"If you follow these instructions, your journey will end well. Remember, go to the west! You will come to a new land, a good land, a land of harmony and hospitality free of bully bugs and gimme bugs, and there you will understand in full. As you travel toward this good land, remember that I will not be far away. I have never been far away.

"One last thing: when you dispute and cannot agree which way to go, Miller the millipede will lead. He will find the way within himself. Let no one despise his words."

And with that the glowing bug receded. He did not turn around and walk away, but drifted slowly backward into the forest until he was just a dot of light. Then he vanished.

While the angelic bug spoke, the four bugs were as immobile as the stone they stood on. They were filled with awe; they only gazed and listened. Not one antenna twitched. Now that he was gone, they looked at each other in amazement.

"The Great Firefly!" said Felicity in an ecstatic voice.

"Firefly?" said the other three in unison.

"It was a millipede!"

"It was an ant!"

"It was a water-skater!"

Each was angry and appalled that the others had not seen the same thing. They called each other "crazy" and "blind" and "stupid" and "idiot" and "liar" and "damned fool" and worse things than that.

They could not agree on what the angel was, but they did agree to follow his instructions. Auntie, however, was shocked by his instruction to follow the lead of Miller, and she threatened not to go unless some kind of a deal were struck.

"Miller"—she forced herself to say his name—"I will follow you only if you agree to ferment my leaves in your backpack."

"Who do you think you are?!" shot back Skeeter. "Carry your own baggage, or eat what comes along!"

But Auntie wouldn't budge, and over Skeeter's hot-headed protest Miller agreed to carry the leaf morsels. The journey was delayed half a day while Auntie cut choice leaves and prepared them to ferment in Miller's stuffy backpack.

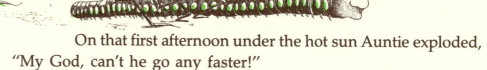

On that first afternoon under the hot sun Auntie exploded, "My God, can't he go any faster!"

"Shut up!" shot back Skeeter, whose temper was at least the equal of Auntie's. "He carries your filthy baggage, and you complain!" The truth is that Skeeter wished Miller wouldn't go quite so fast. Skeeter had never before in his life spent so much time on land, and he found it rough going.

On the second day, as they ate lunch under a rotting log

in a dense forest of pine and oak, they agreed to put aside their suspicions and attempt some kind of dialogue. Auntie, looking up from her scrumptious leaf, said, "What did you all think the angel was talking about?"

"You mean when he said there was something we had to learn from what happened on the rock?" said Felicity.

"That's exactly what I mean," said Auntie.

"He was telling us that the land is full of danger, that there is safety only on water," said Skeeter emphatically as he adjusted the bandage on his bruised left front knee.

"That's your opinion, Twig!" said Auntie. "Don't talk to me about what *is,* talk to me about what you *think* is!"

"His name is not 'Twig,' " cautioned Felicity in a voice as sweet as she could make it.

"Pardon *me*!" said Auntie.

"I'm only reminding you of what the angel said," Felicity said anxiously.

"Since you like opinions so much," said Skeeter then in a voice lilting with malevolence, "I have an *opinion* for you. It is my *opinion* that those disgusting leaves you eat *stink*—stink to high heaven!"

Thus ended their first effort at dialogue.

On the fourth day the four came to a swiftly flowing, gurgling stream. How would they get Miller, who could not swim, across? Miller agreed that Felicity should fly up and down the stream and look for a fallen log to cross. But the firefly could find no passage closer than a day's journey away.

"Too long," said Miller. "We were told to go west."

"It's just a detour," pleaded Auntie.

"It's too far out of the way," said Miller. " The angel said *west*, and that's where we're going."

"We'll get back on course. Don't be so literal-minded, Miller," Auntie said.

But Miller trusted his untutored instincts more than Auntie's liberal interpretation of what the angel might have meant by "west." And as the ant sulked and chafed, Miller formulated his plan. He would float himself across on a leaf with Skeeter navigating. It would be dangerous, not at all like floating on a still pond. Moreover, Skeeter had seen one of those giant waterbugs that can eat a small frog in one sucking swallow.

No, this would not be easy, but Miller trusted the angel. Skeeter then chose a leaf, and Miller crawled aboard. At the last second Auntie, who could swim with difficulty but preferred not to, agreed to join Miller on the leaf. The three of them pushed out into the current.

No one had imagined what danger lurked in that stream—not from water bugs or other bullies, but from the water itself. As soon as the leaf caught the current, Skeeter lost control. He had the strength to push, but he could not keep the raft on course. Around and around they spun, down the stream they were swept, Skeeter clinging and trying frantically to navigate, Miller and Auntie hanging on for dear life.

Suddenly an overhanging branch loomed dead ahead, its ends dangling in the stream. "We're going to crash!" yelled Auntie. "Watch out!"

The boat smashed into the leafy twigs, capsized, then disappeared under the swift stream. Miller caught hold of one of the twigs and climbed up to safety, but Auntie was swept downstream.

Skeeter saw at once what he had to do. Free of his burden, he took out after Auntie. Now he was in his element, and he stroked like the master that he was. He would show that smart-aleck ant! He quickly caught up with her. "Grab hold!" he screamed as he held out his front right leg. "Eeek!" he said as he felt the ant's pincers

close eerily around him. His flesh crawled, and the hair on top of his head seemed to stand straight out.

That night they camped beside the stream at the base of the tree whose branches swam in the stream—the tree that had capsized the raft. And for the first time they did not just go to sleep without a word as night fell. It was Auntie who spoke.

"Now I know what it is we learned on the stone. Now I know what the angel was talking about. Friendship. We are friends. Don't you see?"

"Friends?" said Skeeter, but without sneering.

No one said another word, for they were too exhausted

to agree or disagree. But each in his own way relived the river crossing in his dreams. And each discovered that what Auntie had said had at least a little truth in it.

For two weeks more they traveled over low piney hills and shallow valleys darkened by oak, alder, willow, sorrel, dogwood and sycamore. There were many more watercourses to cross, but none as difficult as the first. They began talking to each other as they walked. They began to trust each other and learn from each other. Sometimes they even got excited about what they learned. They even learned to joke.

"What do you say, Skeeter? Are those bruises illusions?" laughed Miller, who turned out to be a tease.

Poor Skeeter was always tripping. There were sticks to cross, scuppernong vines to thread through, and slippery pine needles to tiptoe over. He was simply not cut out for the work. Once

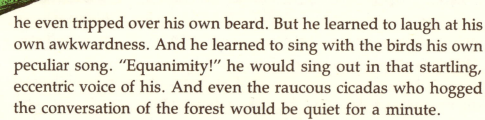

he even tripped over his own beard. But he learned to laugh at his own awkwardness. And he learned to sing with the birds his own peculiar song. "Equanimity!" he would sing out in that startling, eccentric voice of his. And even the raucous cicadas who hogged the conversation of the forest would be quiet for a minute.

Strange to say, Auntie had become genuinely fond of Skeeter. It wasn't only the fact that Skeeter had saved her from drowning that endeared him to her. It was rather that she had at last come to see in him a wit the equal of her own. He made her think as no one ever had before.

On one occasion he forced her out of hiding—out of hiding from herself. He got her to admit that she had called out to something from another world, a greater world, a better world, on that "death ride" down the stream. "You never knew before then what you really were," he said. "You never knew your own nature. And do you know why? I bet you can't tell me."

"Why?" she said.

"Because you ants never leave each other alone long enough to discover what you are. You have never known solitude."

She took this criticism without a word of protest.

One day they came out onto a sun-baked field of corn. For two days they walked on dirt under a glaring blue sky. At the end of the second day they met Cochran.

Sometimes a bug would ask the four travelers what they were doing. It was such a strange procession: a millipede, an ant, a firefly beetle, and a bedraggled, bandaged, bearded bug that most of them couldn't identify.

"We are headed for the Good Land," one of the four would usually answer.

"What's that?" the inquirer would say.

"It's a place of harmony and hospitality without any bully bugs or gimme bugs."

"Oh," the inquirer would say. And then typically he would walk away without another word.

But Cochran was different. This was especially strange because he came from a family of gimme bugs.

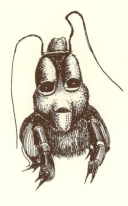

Cochran was a cockroach who lived in a huge old live oak next to a farmhouse and wore a hat in the latest style. Every night he and his family pillaged the house for food. They were never disappointed, and not once in his life had he come across the chemicals of the humans that the elders of his tribe warned him about.

But Cochran was not happy. And when he happened to see the strange procession of misfits parade by his oak tree one afternoon under a high hot sun, and after he asked the usual question and got the standard answer, he asked if he could go along too.

"But you are a gimme bug!" objected Auntie. "Why should you want to go to a place where there are none of your kind?"

Blades of cool grass towered over the four as they paused to drink water droplets produced by those human contraptions

known as sprinklers. For a long time the cockroach said nothing. He seemed to be thinking hard about something. Finally he said, "I am not a gimme bug."

"What do you mean?" said Auntie.

"I am not happy with all my possessions and pleasures. They are not enough. I don't know what else there could be worth having, but I'll try anything. And there is so much bickering at home....I really would like to go with you."

"Then come along," said Miller.

"No!" screamed Auntie. "What—what—?" But then she remembered what the angel had said: Miller was in charge. She said no more, but loathed the idea of traveling with this foul-smelling pariah.

"What is your name?" said Miller with a peculiar cheer. He secretly relished the prospect of traveling with a bug lower, for once, in everyone's estimation than he.

"Cochran," said the newcomer.

So now they were five.

One day under a fierce July sun after a month on the road, the five came to a railroad embankment. The side of the embankment was loose gray gravel, jagged and hot. It would be a difficult and dangerous crossing.

"Will you join me," asked Felicity, "in a prayer?"

They all touched antennae, as Felicity had taught them, and asked the Great Parent to protect them. Auntie secretly scorned the idea of a Great Parent who loved each of them. She was willing to admit that there might be something greater than she, something much greater, greater even than the angel they had all seen, but she couldn't be convinced that it loved *her*, Auntie, one insignificant ant among trillions.

"Now we are protected," Felicity confidently declared.

"Aren't you going to fly a reconnaissance?" Skeeter asked.

"Yes, aren't you?" said Miller. "There's got to be a better place than this."

"Trust the Great Parent!" Felicity sang out in her most musical voice.

36

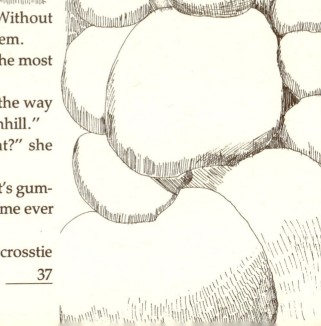

Up the huge mountain of gravel they climbed. It was slow, hot going, and Skeeter was almost delirious by the time he reached the top of the embankment.

As they rested in the slim shadow of one of the tarry crossties that supported the burning rails, Felicity got a sudden bright idea. "We've got to get Skeeter off this gravel," she said. Without consulting anyone, she flitted up to the crosstie above them.

"Careful!" shouted Auntie, who of all the five had the most experience as a walker.

"It's hot," Felicity called, "but its flat. It reaches all the way across to the other side, and it looks like the rest is downhill."

But Auntie was not impressed. "Are you all right?" she hollered up anxiously.

Then Felicity realized something was wrong. "It's—it's gummy up here....I—I think I'm—I'm stuck!" And for the first time ever the other bugs heard fear in Felicity's voice.

Cochran gallantly crawled up the sticky side of the crosstie

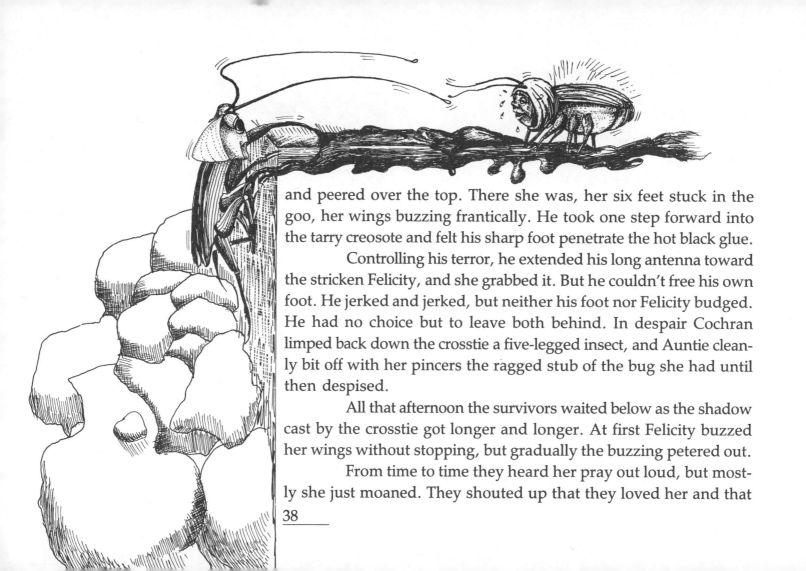

and peered over the top. There she was, her six feet stuck in the goo, her wings buzzing frantically. He took one step forward into the tarry creosote and felt his sharp foot penetrate the hot black glue.

Controlling his terror, he extended his long antenna toward the stricken Felicity, and she grabbed it. But he couldn't free his own foot. He jerked and jerked, but neither his foot nor Felicity budged. He had no choice but to leave both behind. In despair Cochran limped back down the crosstie a five-legged insect, and Auntie cleanly bit off with her pincers the ragged stub of the bug she had until then despised.

All that afternoon the survivors waited below as the shadow cast by the crosstie got longer and longer. At first Felicity buzzed her wings without stopping, but gradually the buzzing petered out.

From time to time they heard her pray out loud, but mostly she just moaned. They shouted up that they loved her and that if she could just hang on until it got dark...but no one really believed in the hope they held out. By the time the crickets and frogs took up their evening chorus, Felicity was quiet.

That night they camped next to the crosstie. Since they had nothing else to eat, Auntie parceled out the last morsel of specially treated leaf from Miller's backpack. But Miller himself was too dazed to eat.

"Eat up, Miller," said the ever-practical Auntie. "You'll need to be strong tomorrow."

But the stricken millipede just stared ahead vacantly.

"What's wrong, Miller?" said Auntie.

He answered her in a voice so soft and ghostly that Auntie shivered: "The angel said that if we obeyed all the instructions, all would be well. What did we do wrong? And where is she now?...Where is she now?...Where is she now?" Suddenly the whole length of his hose-like body shuddered, and he began to sob soundlessly.

"Maybe she's where she always said she'd be—in heaven," said Auntie, gulping as she said these extraordinary words.

"I don't believe in heaven," sobbed Miller. "She's just dead, that's all."

The next morning Cochran climbed up the side of the crosstie again to check on Felicity. There she was, just as he had last seen her, except that now she was as still as stone. The ends of her antennae had drooped, and they too were stuck in the tar. They quivered in the wind like a tightly strung bow.

As Skeeter passed over the jagged gravel and under the two rails, he remembered that Felicity had lost her life in trying to spare him this short walk. He told himself that she was a good girl, and he admitted for the first time that he actually had liked her.

The days passed. Ditches, furrows, puddles, streams, thick grass, and tricky forest floors—these demons of the earth—assailed them again and again.

Cochran was the first to lose faith. "How far *is* the Good Land?" he said one day. He began to grumble about the food he had to eat. He missed the junk food that the humans consumed and the delicious sugars and fats they left behind in their kitchens.

One day they found themselves approaching one of the colonies that the humans lived in. Now Cochran could smell the food he so missed, and it almost drove him crazy. In the evening twilight of the thirty-ninth day of the journey, the smell of cherry pie baking sent him into a frenzy, and he could bear it no longer.

He wept as he said goodbye to Auntie, Skeeter, and especially Miller. He said he knew he was doing the wrong thing, but he just couldn't stop himself.

"If only I could be more sure that there really *was* a Good Land!" Cochran said.

"There is!" said Miller. "It can't be far ahead now. Don't give up!"

"Equanimity," Skeeter chimed in. "Equanimity!"

But that evening Cochran waddled away.

The truth is that Cochran had dared to ask the very question that the rest of them had been asking themselves secretly for some time. The angel and the land of harmony and hospitality that he promised had come to seem very far away.

They reminded each other of the way the angel had appeared to each of them in his own guise on that distant day, but now he seemed no more real than a vivid but ancient dream.

"Where in the devil *is* the Good Land?" said Auntie out loud for the first time.

"No one said it would be easy to find," said Skeeter.

"There is something up ahead," said Miller, "something different, something that—I can't explain it—my legs are telling me—a rumbling of the earth. I've sensed it for the last half hour. Maybe—maybe it's the Good Land."

They walked on, and now they began to confront the things that the humans ride in. Two human feet in those clattering things they call shoes walked by. Then it began to rain hard, and Miller, Auntie, and Skeeter took refuge in a woodpile next to a human house. But the pile was filled with black widow spiders.

"Look out, Skeeter!"

Auntie's yell was a second too late, and Skeeter's right front leg plunged through the deadly web.

Skeeter pulled back as hard as he could, but he couldn't break loose. Then Auntie crept up close to the point of contact. "Stay still or you'll get me stuck too!" she screamed.

"*I* didn't move!" said Skeeter.

And it was true: Skeeter didn't move. Something else made the web quiver.

42

"Auntie!" screamed Miller.

Auntie turned around and looked up into the shadows to see a huge bulbous spider flexing her muscles. "Get out of here, ant!" came a shrill voice poisonous with death. "Leave him to me!"

"Leave me, Auntie, I'm a goner," said Skeeter in a faint, shaking whisper. "Life and death—what are they but illusions?"

But Auntie didn't have time for philosophy. In one terrific motion she bit off Skeeter's leg at the knee.

Skeeter screamed in agony while Auntie gripped his middle leg and pulled him back out of the crack into the rain. "You old fool!" she said. "What are you screaming about—an illusion?"

That night, as the strange rumbling that Miller felt with his sensitive legs continued, the three bugs looked at each other and felt something they had never felt before. "You weird old coot," said Auntie to Skeeter, "I would have missed you."

They had bedded down in the middle of a lawn far from the creepy nocturnal haunts of bully bugs and gimme bugs. The night was warm, and the stars shone as innocently as they had half

a lifetime ago over the Green Fern Forest.

In his peculiar jittery voice from another world, Skeeter began to philosophize. "Strange. Very strange. Here in this hostile world, my only friends an ant and a millipede, I discover that it is good to be alive. Look up there. Beautiful!"

Skeeter had never said anything like this before. Never had he talked of beauty and friendship, but only of equanimity and illusion.

"Do you mean it?" said Miller in his country drawl.

"Mean what?"

"That I am your friend?"

" 'Friend'? Did I say that?"

"You did."

"Then why do you ask?"

"And Auntie too?"

"Auntie?" (It was the second time in his life he had ever said her name, and the first time had been in anger.) "The old girl saved my life."

"Don't give reasons," said Miller. "Talk feelings. Do you feel friendship for her?"

Skeeter turned toward Auntie and looked her up and down. He squinted into the night and peered into her bespectacled eyes. He stroked his disheveled graying beard twice. Then he smiled at her.

The next day, the fortieth of the journey, dawned full of promise. Even with Skeeter in pain and limping, the bugs made good time. By noon they had crossed the yards of thirty human dwellings and three paved streets without any mishaps.

Then they saw what it was that Miller had been sensing with his legs: two strips of asphalt full of speeding demons that carried the humans to their destinations. Auntie, Miller, and Skeeter felt their hearts drop, for they had convinced themselves that the journey was about to end.

"Maybe the Good Land is on the other side," said Miller.

Skeeter could make out an unbroken line of trees on the far side of the demonway. What might it be hiding? Even Auntie

let herself hope again. But in the heart of each was an altogether new fear. Now they saw clearly what made the ground shake and what Miller felt with his sensitive feet. How would they escape being squashed by these screaming demons?

As dark clouds came up out of the east behind them, Miller, Auntie, and Skeeter crossed a field and rafted over shallow water standing in a ditch. Just as they were climbing up to the edge of the demonway, which was flat and straight, the clouds broke. The three bugs had no place to go, and the huge drops pounded them into the ground and knocked them silly.

It crossed Auntie's mind that this might be the final trial before the gateway to the Good Land opened, but a crash of thunder made her think of things closer to hand—like those rolling black rubber paws that squash bugs into shapeless shadows. How the demons did roar!

Now they really missed Felicity. They needed her to fly up and down the road and look for a drainage pipe under the pavement. "We'll just have to wait for a lull," said Auntie. And it was true that every now and then there was a lull in the traffic. They decided to cross one at a time to the median, regroup, then repeat the maneuver to the far side. If only they could see farther!

They experimented to learn whether Skeeter's eyes or Miller's feet could better predict safe periods for crossing. They soon learned that there was no such thing as a truly safe period. Miller in particular was just too slow. They would simply have to trust the angel to protect them and take their chances.

Now they missed Felicity in another way. As the mammoth engines of destruction whooshed by with the force of a hurricane, each bug felt the need to pray as Felicity had tried to teach them. "Do you think there really is a Great Parent?" said Miller.

"The angel never mentioned him," said Auntie.

"Felicity was so sure, she trusted him so much, but look what happened to her," said Miller.

"I trust the angel," said Auntie, "not the Great Parent."

"Then let's pray to the angel," said Miller.

This they did. They prayed that he would take them safely to the Good Land. They reminded him of his promise, and they assured him that they had done all he asked them to do, just in case he didn't already know.

"Who is going first?" Auntie asked Miller.

"I am." Miller held out his antennae and touched those of Auntie and then those of Skeeter. "The Good Land!" he said.

Miller checked his backpack, curled himself around, and walked up to the edge of the demonway, with Auntie and Skeeter behind him. By now the sun was sitting on top of the trees on the far side of the road. Was that an omen? And if it was, was it a good or a bad one? Miller waited...and waited...and waited.

"Now!" said Skeeter.

Miller got his seventy-odd legs working as fast as he could. Farther and farther out he went. He was almost halfway across the road when he began to feel that familiar vibration in his legs.

"Hurry! Hurry!" came a scream from behind him.

Miller looked to his left. A huge roaring demon was bearing down on him with its rolling weapons of destruction screaming across the black asphalt. Help me, Great Parent! he thought to himself. Help me! Then a great whirlwind engulfed him. There was something like a sting, just a faint sting that tingled in every nerve of his body for a single darkening instant. Then there was nothing.

Auntie and Skeeter looked in horror at the spot where they had last seen Miller. There was nothing, absolutely nothing there. They looked to see if he had been blown down the road by the wind. "Miller?" they cried. "Miller?"

Then Auntie began to curse the angel. She shrieked and sobbed and smashed her glasses on the rocky shoulder. "You were right all along!" she screamed at Skeeter. "It *is* all an illusion! The Great Parent, the Good Land, even the angel! We must have imagined him!"

"I don't think so," said Skeeter. Skeeter did not speak like a bug who had just lost his dear friend. There was a tenseness in his voice, but there was not even a hint of mourning.

"You monster!" screamed Auntie. "You unfeeling monster! You and your damned equanimity!"

"We will see," said Skeeter.

And with that he limped up to the edge of the asphalt, looked once to his left, and started across.

"Be careful!" he heard Auntie cry.

He got as far as the white line in the middle and waited there while demons screamed past on both sides of him. He looked back and saw Auntie standing up on three legs like a tripod. Poor Auntie, she couldn't see a thing without her glasses. What chance did she have? Skeeter decided to go back and lead her across. Across to the Good Land.

"I'm coming back for you!" he yelled.

"No, you old fool!" she answered, "I can take care of myself! Keep going!"

But Skeeter knew better, and on he came. So did something else, a bright red demon pulling a gleaming silver weapon as big as one of the human's houses. Skeeter heard it, then saw it, then—whoooooosh!

"Skeeter?...Skeeter?...Skeeter?... *Skeeter*!" But the only answer Auntie got was the twitter of a mockingbird singing in some faraway field or forest that she couldn't see.

In rage and despair Auntie flung herself out onto the road. She did not look right or left, she did not calculate. She kept walking straight ahead, both anticipating and dreading the pulverizing squash that would mercifully end it all. She saw nothing, heard nothing. Then suddenly, to her astonishment, she found herself on the median.

Not knowing what to think anymore, she walked across a narrow field of cut grass to the other road. Now the demons were screaming at her from the opposite direction. For some reason she took heart. She began to care whether she lived or died.

She began to think, to remember, to reason. She remembered that at night the humans slept. Wouldn't their demons therefore have to sleep too? She would wait, yes, she would wait—wait until it was very, very late. Then she would cross over. Who knows, maybe Skeeter knew something she didn't know. Maybe the Good Land really was on the other side of the tree line. Maybe she alone was destined to get there. A determined new hope rose within her.

Just as she had suspected, the demons slept with their masters. Far fewer of them prowled at night, and these were usually the big ones that roared and that you could hear far away. Auntie waited and wept for Skeeter through that interminable night.

Then, shortly before first light, there was not a sound to be heard from any direction. It was if she were back home in the Green Fern Forest with only crickets and frogs to disturb the silence. She took a deep breath...and hurried across. Soon she felt rough gravel under her feet, then grass. She had made it, and for a moment she felt a wild, giddy, exhilarating thrill.

She had saved herself with her own wits, just as the elders back in the nest had taught her to do when she was but a girl. She had depended on no one else, not the Great Parent, not even the angel. Now she would find out if the angel had told the truth, she would find out if the Good Land really did lie on the other side of the tree line. And if it did not, she would root around until she found another nest, have new glasses made, and make a new home. She would be all right either way. And what stories she would tell! And what wisdom she would impart!

Auntie had not forgotten her friends; she still carried a heavy heart. But as she swam across stagnant water in the narrow ditch on the far side of the demonway, she thought only of the future. Either way it would be all right!

She could not see distinctly, but she could tell that she had entered the forest. What lay on the other side? What, if anything? She bounded forward. She hadn't slept all night, but she did not feel tired.

Suddenly Auntie felt something strange and sticky under her right front foot. She stopped. Something deep and primeval in-side her told her that she was in mortal danger, but she pushed the warning aside, and refused to believe it. She applied her pincers to the sticky stuff and tried to free her foot. But instead she found that her pincers only got stuck.

Deep down inside her voice said "spider, spider," but Auntie pretended to herself that she didn't hear it.

Then she looked up, and what she saw in vague outline

paralyzed her with fright. A huge bully bug—a spider with great horned talons and a green-striped fuzzy black belly—lurched forward. Auntie pulled back with an unnatural strength born of terror, but the sticky stuff would not let go.

"Ha ha ha ha ha!" laughed the fiendish spider.

Then Auntie began snapping her jaws. "Snap, snap!" they rang out in the forest.

The spider stopped for a minute, then laughed all the louder, "Ha ha ha! I'll take care of that!"

All the while respecting her powerful jaws and keeping his distance, the spider began slowly wrapping Auntie up in his web. Auntie watched in utter horror as the sticky stuff poured out of the spider's guts and wrapped around her tighter and tighter. Still she kept up her game fight, and the forest rang out with "snap, snap!" Once the spider got too close and she severed one of his feet with a single bite.

This enraged him, and he swore that he would eat her bit by bit, drag it out, let her die of pain.

Auntie more and more began to look like a cocoon, but still her jaws snapped. How long could she fight? She could barely keep her jaws between the cannibal and the juicy hinder parts that he

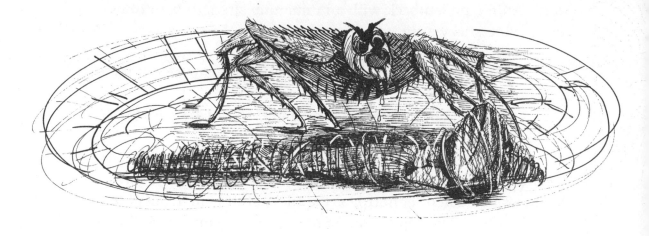

planned to eat first.

Then she could turn no more. She lay still, exhausted, not even snapping her jaws. And as the first light of the rising red sun split the forest and made the web shimmer, Auntie called out to the Great Parent.

Then she felt an excruciating, tearing pain in her upper thorax, and blacked out.

THE GOOD LAND

"Auntie!" said Miller and Skeeter as they stood on the smooth stone beside the pond under the ferns in the Green Fern Forest. They smiled at her as she crawled up to them. They held out their antennae for her to touch. "Welcome home! Welcome home!" they said. "We've been waiting for you!" Then Felicity came crawling up to her too, but there was a look of self-doubt and even tragedy on her face.

"What—is—this?" Auntie stammered. "Where—where am—I?" She was utterly bewildered.

"Auntie!" said a strange but thrilling voice from—from— then she saw him. He hovered winglessly over the stone—like....

"Who—what—who are you?" said Auntie.

"You don't recognize me?" said the stranger, who glowed

all over and resembled no bug Auntie had ever seen before.

Auntie stared hard at the awe-inspiring bug. There was something about him that made her think she knew him. Yet at the same time she was quite sure she never had seen a bug that looked anything like him. Then a long-forgotten memory stirred deep within her, and she recognized him. She recognized him not by his looks, but by a certain feel she had in his presence.

"The angel!" she said. "The Guardian!"

Then all the events of her life flooded back into her memory. She remembered the agony of being trapped in the spider's web, the demons that roared up and down the demonway, the stream that swept her away, the apparition of the ant-angel on the rock, the ambush, the collision with Miller on that fateful day in another world....Another world, yes!

Then she remembered how she had felt certain that she would die. She remembered seeing that monstrous bully bug's gleaming eyes and smelling his sour breath as he bore down on her. How far away it seemed; yet it seemed like only—only minutes ago! What was happening?

"Am I—am I—dead?" she asked sheepishly.

" You don't look very dead to me!" said Skeeter as excitedly as ever. It was as if nothing had happened.

"But I'm sure I—how did I get back here? And what happened to the Good Land?" said Auntie.

"This is the Good Land," said the angel.

"This?" said Auntie. She looked around her, then back at the angel's glowing face. "This? This?...you're—you're joking."

"No, Auntie, I am not joking."

"This is the Good Land? *This?* But—but this can't be!"

"Auntie...."

"It's the same old place!... We didn't even have to move. What was the journey for anyway? All that suffering—for nothing. I can't believe it. We're right back where we started. I—I want an explanation. I demand an explanation!" Then she glowered at the august angel. "How about it, Glowbones? You lied to us! You *lied!*"

Miller and Felicity gasped at the insult, but the angel only smiled. "Be at peace, Auntie," he said.

"I am not at peace! For forty days we journeyed. We suffered horribly. As soon as I learned to care for my odd friends here, they died—picked off one by one right before my eyes. You took us away from our families, our natural friends, our own kind.

"And for what? For something you say was right under our noses all along? I can't believe it! We trusted you, and you made fools out of us! And you ask me to be at peace?"

"Are you finished, Auntie? Will you now listen to me?" said the angel.

Auntie simmered down as she looked into the calm glowing face of the Guardian.

"Does Auntie speak for the rest of you?" he said, looking

at the others. "Do you feel the same way? Have you, too, wondered what the journey was for, and why you had to suffer?"

"I think I know the answer," said Skeeter, always the most philosophical of the four. But Miller and Felicity said nothing.

"Go ahead, Skeeter," said the angel.

"The journey taught me to respect nature. Spending all my time on that peaceful pond, I passed the world off as an illusion. I did not take it seriously, I scorned it. I did not see its—its solidity, its reality. I would not admit it had any power over me. I stayed aloof from it, from its inhabitants. I didn't let myself care for it, care about making it better. I didn't *love* it. I was...selfish.

"But I learned, learned every time I stumbled and bruised my knee, to respect it. And I learned to depend on my friends here, and finally to care about them."

"Very good, Skeeter!" said the angel. "A rare bug it is that understands as much as you. Were you a philosopher back in the old world?"

Skeeter did not see the twinkle in the angel's eye, and for an instant he felt that familiar temper of his flare up again. "A philosopher?" he said. "That surely would have been the ruin of me! I meditated!" Then he realized he had made a mistake. "But, of course, you already know that," he said sheepishly.

The angel looked lovingly at Skeeter. "Yes, I do. I have followed each of your careers with great interest." Then he turned to Felicity. "And what about you, Felicity?"

"Me?...I don't know," said Felicity, who seemed to speak out of some secret sorrow.

"Then I will tell you." Now the angel turned his loving, accepting smile at the crestfallen firefly. "You depended too much on the Great Parent to protect you, Felicity. Think back to the event that cost you your life. Do you remember how reckless you were? Even though you had wings, you did not bother to inspect the route. You trusted the Great Parent to take care of you, no matter what you did.

"But that is not how the Great Parent operates, Felicity. He expects you to do all in your power to take care of yourself—and your friends. Do you remember how Skeeter asked you to fly a reconnaissance before crossing those rocky tracks? And how you refused, and what a terrible price he paid climbing those burning rocks? And Cochran...."

"No! No!" Felicity suddenly screamed, and she wept so bitterly that she shook.

The angel waited for her to subside, then added, "If you had trusted the Great Parent a little less to solve all your problems, and relied more on yourself, you would then have discovered a level crossing within a half hour's walk. All would have been different."

Felicity's compassionate round eyes were red with grief. She hung her head in despair, and the light in her belly bleeped on and off out of control.

"But you have learned your lesson, Felicity, learned it so dramatically that you are likely never to forget it. And that is the whole point of life in the old world," said the Angel. . . . "Miller, go to her. Go and comfort her."

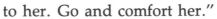

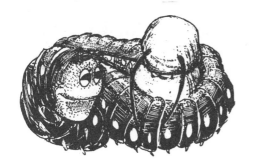

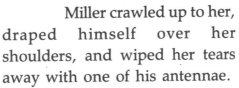

Miller crawled up to her, draped himself over her shoulders, and wiped her tears away with one of his antennae.

" And that brings me to you, Miller," said the angel after

Felicity's sobbing had again subsided. "What did the journey teach you?"

"I am not so clever as Skeeter," said the amiable millipede. "Please, you may tell me."

"Miller, you were so entranced with the world that you could not admit there was any other. Even after seeing me on the rock the first time, it did not seriously occur to you that I was from a different world. Where did you think I had come from?

"As for the Great Parent, you turned him into dumb, mute nature. You refused to see anything behind nature, sustaining nature, holding it in place. Nature, you thought, was enough. Nature was wholly good and would take care of you. If you didn't actually think this, you acted as if you did. You simply never gave a thought to anything higher or better.

"And you were determined never to think about death, even though you lived in a forest of bully bugs that dearly loved the tender flesh of the millipede. Not until the journey did you come to terms with death. You finally learned to put nature into perspective, and you even learned in the end to call out to the Great Parent. You yearned for something greater than nature, and that is why you are here. That is why...."

"I'm beginning to get the picture," Auntie broke in, who by now was in better spirits, "but I still don't understand why you didn't just tell us what we had to know rather than put us through all this hell."

"Auntie," said the angel, "it's been over a thousand years since I was on earth, and even though I've come a long way since then, I still sometimes forget the lessons I learned there. Bugs *forget*. They are much less likely to forget if they have paid dearly for their wisdom. Soon you will understand this. Trust me when I tell you this. But for now...."

"My turn, eh?"

"That's right, Auntie. But first"—the angel turned back to Miller and smiled—"are there any questions, Miller?"

"No," said the chastened millipede.

Then the angel turned to the ant. "By the way, Auntie," he said, "why are you wearing those glasses?"

"Glasses? What...? Where did they come from?"

"I'll explain in a minute, but for now, if you like, throw them away."

"Throw them away?" Auntie took them off and inspected them. Then she happened to look up. "I can—I can seeeeee!" she

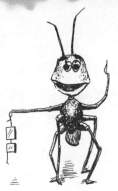

sang. "Farther, farther than ever!"

"You said a moment ago," said the angel, "that the journey took you nowhere, except right back where you came from. Are you so sure of this now?"

Auntie looked around. "It looks the same to me," she said, "except that I can see so much farther!"

The angel chuckled. "Always the skeptic, Auntie! Well, let's see what you have learned. You leaf-cutter ants have an old tradition that puts the Great Parent in the center of your lives. Do you remember being taught this as a girl? But hard work and what you called 'sisterhood' squeezed him out. You even told yourself that 'reason' made the Great Parent an 'unnecessary hypothesis.' So you forgot about him, forgot to give him thanks. You did not exactly deny him, you just forgot about him.

"And in time you became like Miller—so entranced by the solid, gleaming world around you that you denied there was any other. You too had to learn again how to call out to the Great Parent. Auntie, do you remember the last thing you did before you died?"

"So I really am dead?"

"Yes, Auntie, you are dead!" laughed the angel. "Do you remember what you did?"

Auntie thought for a minute. "I called out to the Great Parent?"

"You did indeed. You had at last come to the end of your rope. You could do nothing, absolutely nothing for yourself; for once your wits couldn't save you. You acknowledged this by calling out to the Great Parent. And in the process—don't you see?—you came to see that life is a gift. You did nothing to deserve it, you did not invent it with your wits, you did not reason it out. You were simply given it. You were given it because the Great Parent loves you, and for no other reason."

Auntie, for once, said nothing. For a long time she just stared out over the pond. Then she turned back around, and in a voice almost cheerful she asked, "By the way, why did you put Miller in charge of us on the journey?"

"I'm surprised you haven't figured that out yet. You and Felicity and Skeeter, for all your differences, are insects. Each of you has six legs. But Miller has seventy-four, and you scorned him for it."

"Miller had already learned humility. His life was a string of humiliations, for he was an outsider. That is why I put him in charge, to teach you humility."

For a few seconds no one said anything. A warm breeze caressed the leaves of the forest, and ripples lapped at the shore of the pond. Then Auntie turned to Miller and said, "I'm sorry, Miller." And at that instant a frog croaked loudly from the center of the pond.

At that point Felicity, gentle Felicity, erupted. "I did *not* look down on Miller, *ever*! I did *not* feel superior to him!" And the light in her belly glowed red and seemed to flutter, as if to the beat of her heart.

"Not in the same way as Auntie, that is true," said the angel in a voice at once stern and gentle. "You might remember, though,

68

that you thought him, and Skeeter and Auntie too, unworthy of the Great Parent's love. Do you remember?"

"Well, yes, but—they...."

"They didn't believe in the Firefly Son—is that what you were going to say?" And for the first time there was a hint of reproval in the angel's kindly voice.

"Yes," said Felicity.

"Felicity, you are right in saying that the Great Parent loves the Firefly Son in a special way. And it is true that the Son has great power and helps those who trust in him—especially fireflies, for they turn to him in the greatest numbers.

"But there are no automatic passwords to the Good Land, or to the Great Land beyond. And there is no single belief required before you can enter. To tell you the truth, beliefs, while important, are somewhat secondary. It's what your beliefs draw out of you that counts. Have you loved? Have you disciplined your passions and cravings? Have you conquered timidity and laziness? Character, habits—these, Felicity, these are basic."

Then all the disillusionment that Felicity had felt from the first moment of her arrival in this new country burst the dikes of her heart. "I feel deceived!" she wailed.

"Why is that?" said the angel.

"This can't be the Good Land! I expected something else! Where is the Firefly Son? I thought you were him, but you're—you're just—you're weird! And where are all those who love him? Where are the other fireflies? Am I—am I—in *hell*?"

She almost screamed this last word out, and the angel decided to move quickly to the main point.

"Felicity," he said, "look out there on the pond."

Through her tears she looked out, and there to her surprise was a small island. "Where did—where did that come from?" she said shakily.

"I just now put it there."

Felicity's bug-eyes suddenly dried and looked as if they might swell out of her head. She said in a voice hushed with awe, "Who—who are you?"

The angel laughed gently. Then he said, "A thousand or so years ago I was a bug like yourself, and I too prowled the old world. . . . You don't like the island out there, Felicity? Then remove it. Yes, that's the thing to do. Remove it."

"What did you say?"

"Remove it, Felicity."

"Remove it? What—what do you mean?"

"Exactly what I said. Remove it, Felicity."

"Remove it? . . . How?"

"By willing it away. Concentrate, then tell it to go away. Tell it, Felicity. Tell it."

She concentrated, told it, and, sure enough, it disappeared.

"Felicity," said the angel, "the Firefly Son and his Kingdom are as far away as your will. You can get there as easily as you just willed away that island. But be patient a little longer. There is some unfinished business here first. Will you be patient, dear Felicity?"

"Do you mean I can...?" She couldn't continue, but a brilliant green-gold light began to throb in her belly.

"Yes, Felicity, but will you wait a little while longer? Please. Then I will tell you how to join him. Trust me, Felicity."

Then the angel turned to Auntie and said, "A little while ago, Auntie, you doubted this was the Good Land. You thought it was the same old Green Fern Forest. What do you think now?"

"I don't—I don't know," stammered Auntie, whose amazement over the disappearance of the island had been greater than Felicity's.

"Auntie," said the angel, "I made it look like the Green Fern Forest so you would feel at home when you arrived, and because...."

"You mean you could have made it look like something entirely different?" said Auntie.

"That's right," said the angel, "but here we are—standing on this familiar old stone.... There is another reason for this. Can any of you guess it?"

Nobody said anything. A breeze blew in across the pond, and clouds hid the sun.

"I want each of you to remember," said the angel, "what I asked you to do back in the old world, when I first talked to you from this stone. Do you remember what it was?"

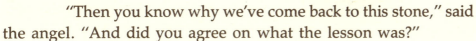

"We remember," said Auntie. "The lesson. We had to learn the lesson."

"Then you know why we've come back to this stone," said the angel. "And did you agree on what the lesson was?"

The four bugs looked at each other. It was clear that they hadn't agreed.

"Can you agree now?" said the angel.

Auntie looked first at Miller. "Miller," she said, "what do you think...?"

"Auntie, that's not necessary," the angel interrupted. "You don't have to talk. Just attune yourself. Miller has opened his mind to you. See what's there. Go ahead, Auntie, see what's there."

For a second Auntie looked at the angel as if he might be

joking, but then she said, "How do I do it?"

"By *doing* it, that's all!" laughed the angel, heartily. "Go ahead, Auntie! See for yourself."

Auntie shook her head, then looked at Miller and concentrated. "Yes! Yes!" she said after a moment. "Yes! Yes!"

"And how about Skeeter and Felicity?"

Auntie attuned herself first to one, then the other. After a moment she said, "Yes, we do now. Felicity and I didn't agree at first, but we worked it out. Yes, we agree, more or less. It was what I suspected all along."

"It was what you tried to tell us from the beginning," said Miller, significantly.

"What was that?" said the angel.

"Can I think it to you?" said Miller with a yuk and a great big country boy's smile.

"You could, but it will turn out a bit fuzzy if you do. I just wanted to give you a taste of what was possible. For now, go ahead and speak it."

"OK," said Miller. "The ambush by the bully bug and his

girl friend, and the way we all reacted, taught me that we shouldn't choose our friends according to the way they look."

"And we shouldn't exclude bugs," Auntie chimed in, "on the basis of what they believe."

"The Great Parent doesn't have favorites!" said Skeeter in the manner of an oracle.

Now everyone turned to Felicity to see what she might say. "What did you learn, Felicity?" said the angel.

"I guess—that I have more allies in this world than I ever dreamed," she said sheepishly.

"By the way, Felicity, was Cochran an ally?" Auntie asked.

"Cochran?" she said in surprise. "I—I don't know."

Auntie turned to the angel for help. "Cochran was a cockroach we met on our...."

"I know all about him," said the angel. "You will be surprised to learn that Cochran was here two days ago. Not here on this stone, but in this country. He joined us less than an hour after he left you—he was gassed by a human as he filled his belly with the sugar he craved so much."

"Oh, poor Cochran!" said Felicity.

"Are you saying," asked Auntie, "that gimme bugs come

here, too? Cochran was a cockroach, you know."

"Gimme bug? Cochran? How you judge by appearances, Auntie! No, they have their own place, not a very nice one, I'm afraid, where they have to go to get strong medicine until they are well. But Cochran was not a true gimme bug, so we brought him up here for a trial. Unfortunately, he was not happy here."

"So what happened to him?" said Auntie.

"Look and see!" said the angel with a twinkle in his eye.

"Where?" said Auntie, looking all around her.

"No, Auntie, look within! Then you will see him. Concentrate. Think of Cochran and wish to be near him."

Auntie closed her eyes and concentrated on Cochran....
"What!" she said after a moment. "He's—he's—he's a leaf-cutter ant!
He's just a baby! And that's my old nest! There are my sisters!...
What's he?—what's he?—I don't understand!"

"Auntie, did you ever guess how much he admired you?
He admired your industry, your energy, your intelligence."

"Cochran?"

"Yes, Auntie. When he was sure he wanted to go back to
the old world, he asked to go back as an ant. And I arranged for
him to be born into your very nest."

"I don't believe it!" said the amazed Auntie. "Just look at
him! Or rather—her." Then she suddenly looked up at the angel
and said, "Can I go back too?"

"You? Auntie, I'm surprised!" And he laughed in that un-
canny, resonant way of his that made Auntie's antennae hum. "Actually, I don't think you'll want to when you get to your destina-
tion. I have big plans for you, Auntie. For each of you."

The angel looked at each of them significantly, and as he
did so the sun came back out and a breeze whirred through the
magical ferns.

"I am the guardian spirit of the kingdom on earth that you

came from. My name, even if it could be spoken in your language, would mean nothing to you, and my true form would be hidden from you if I assumed it.

"I come from a region far beyond. You will someday dwell in it if you choose, but it is now far beyond your grasp. What adventures lie ahead of you! But now there is work to be done. Even I have to work. Even the Great Parent works, but his work is pure joy, pure delight.

"The Good Land is not a place free of struggles and hardship. Just as there are lessons to be learned below, so there are those to be learned here—here at this lowest level of the Good Land. There is none more important than the lesson you have learned—learned better than any bugs that have ever come to this country from below.

"What is that lesson? The one that you learned on the stone and during the journey, the one we just talked about, the very same. This is a land of many kingdoms, but seldom do bugs from one kingdom visit another. In theory they understand, but they don't really feel what is at last clear to each of you: that you are all brothers and sisters, that each of your kingdoms has its own treasure trove of wisdom to give to its kindred kingdoms, and that there is joy in opening your arms ever wider and wider.

"Each of you is uniquely wise. You have been chosen by me to teach your kingdoms. You will be apostles of a more expansive love than has ever been known here before. If you succeed in your mission, what now takes a thousand years to accomplish will take only a hundred. On your shoulders rests the future joy and advancement of trillions of bugs.

"Make no mistake, this will be hard work. Crusty old fuddy-duddies will rise up and try to frustrate you. Persevere when they do. Remember that they, above all others, need your help.

"They are basically well-meaning, or they wouldn't be here. Their narrow thinking habits were learned on earth, just as yours were. They were taught by their elders that their species or hive or family was superior to all others. They assumed without examination that their ancient traditions and customs were the only valid ones. They came to believe that they alone were wise. Be patient with them. You were once exactly like them! Be patient.

"Last, help each other. From time to time the four of you should fashion with your minds a beautiful park for meeting. Fill it with flowering trees, lilied ponds, grassy hillocks, rushing waterfalls, and warm winds. Relive with each other the struggles and perils that brought you together and taught you to depend on each

other for your very lives.

"Celebrate the love that you now feel for each other. And bring with you as many from your kingdoms as will come. Let them see what friends you are. Let them see the joy in your faces when you meet. Let them feel the happiness in your hearts when you greet each other with antennae touching. Show them how you delight in the excellence of each other.

"Celebrate each other. Learn from each other's talents. Learn gratefully, humbly. Make music, sing songs. Make this land glow all over with your love!

"And now, my friends, it is time to say farewell."

Auntie, Skeeter, Miller, and Felicity scarcely knew what to say. They looked at each other and didn't know whether to cry or to laugh. They searched each other's ordinary faces for hidden hints of greatness. They marveled that they could be so special, that they were chosen for such an important mission. In their depths they all felt the same question taking shape: Why me? But not even Auntie put it to words.

"What should we bring with us?" said Miller at last.

"Nothing at all," said the angel.

"Then I won't need my backpack?"

"Never again!" laughed the angel triumphantly.

Miller started to nudge it up toward his head section by section.

"There is an easier way, Miller," said the angel. "Take it off with your will!"

"Oh," said Miller. And he wished it to be off, and it vanished into thin air.

Then it seemed to all four of them that the angel was mysteriously distant from them, yet there was no sense of his having moved. "When will we meet the Great Parent?" Felicity suddenly called out.

"Would you really like to?" called back the angel.

They all said they would.

Then again without any sense of movement, the angel was

in their midst. And as they looked at him, he grew—grew without seeming to grow—gigantic. His face seemed to suck them up. Passing through the pupil of one of his immense eyes, they hurdled down the cavity of a huge flaming vortex. Gradually a luminous face took shape, and all about them was the most perfect stillness.

The face was so vast that one of its eyelashes was as big as a world; indeed each eyelash was a world. And every time the face blinked its eyes, an eon passed. On the face was a smile, and

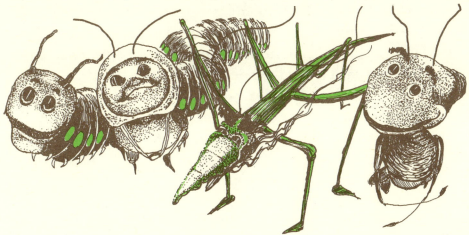

not once during all those eons did the face stop smiling. And out of that smile flowed something that felt like love, but wasn't, for

it was greater than love by the degree that the blazing sun is greater than a twinkling star.

Then, without any sense of movement, the four found themselves back on the stone. They clung to each other, shaking and sobbing. Bliss tinged with terror—that is the only way they could describe what they felt. Their hearts pounded until they seemed on the verge of shattering. Love and terror existing side by side in stupendous, fascinating, but unequal portions—for love finally overcame terror, and each longed to ride down the fiery vortex one more time.

"What you saw," said the angel's voice, "was not really the Great Parent. It is what he looks like distorted by worldly, selfish habits. The more worldly and selfish, the greater the terror when you come into his presence. Had you been bully bugs or gimme bugs you would have turned on your heels and raced back up the vortex in utter terror. The fact that you loved more than feared him is proof of your limited goodness. Still, you are not yet ready for his world. Even I am not.

"When you are, you will see him differently. In fact you will not see him at all. You will participate in him. Seeing is for lower worlds. Be patient, Felicity. The Great Parent will reveal as much of himself—herself—to you as you can stand. Now rest for a while. Sleep if you like. You will soon find out that sleep, like eating, is optional in this country, but for now I recommend it."

The angel was very much himself. Glowing, he smiled across at the four bugs, and they all felt an immense gratitude to him. And they slept dreamlessly until he woke them.

When they woke, the sun had already sunk below the horizon, and a cool twilight hung over the forest. A whippoorwill just across the pond sang its haunting, repetitive melody, and another farther back in the woods answered it like a distant echo.

"Now it is time to go," said the angel. "Each of you should call out to your own kind. You will find that you are expected, that several old friends are waiting for you. But in your joy and celebration, don't forget what I told you—not one word. And now, Felicity, since you appear to be the most eager, you may go first."

Felicity looked at each of her friends and told them that she loved them. "I will miss you," she said. Then she began to cry. "Oh, I feel like I am dying all over again!"

"Get control of yourself, Felicity," said the angel. "A great mission has been given to you. It calls for courage."

"The Firefly Son will help me," she said. Then she sucked in her breath and calmed herself. Tears were drying on her cheeks as she closed her eyes and called out to the Mansion of Fireflies. Then she was gone. She vanished like a rainbow when the sun goes behind the cloud. And even the imperturbable Skeeter felt water gathering in his squinty eyes.

In rapid succession Miller, Skeeter, and Auntie rode the winds of this strange new world to their respective kingdoms, until the angel was left alone on the stone. Then he too vanished, and with him the stone, the pond, the forest, and the crimson sky itself. Not even the whippoorwills sang.

86

And far away, but no farther than the next thought, Auntie, the ever-inquisitive Auntie, alone at last after a jubilant homecoming, wondered if the whippoorwills had been real or just part of the landscape that the angel had fashioned for their benefit. Suddenly she

missed their haunting song; she longed to hear it one more time. And as she looked out into the fabulously starry night of her mysterious new land with its stange new laws, she discovered that she, though merely an ant, could herself sing like the whippoorwill.

Acknowledgments

I thank Francis Vanderwall, S.J., theologian at Spring Hill College in Mobile, Alabama, and author of *Water in the Wilderness*, for suggestions that were crucial to the final form of the book; to Mary Cameron Ernest of Mobile for perceptive criticisms of an earlier manuscript; to Dr. Alvin Tanabe, an entomologist at California State College, Bakersfield, for some expert advice (sometimes ignored) about the habits and ways of insects; to Mrs. N. Q. ("Dolly") Adams of Mobile for letting me use her summer home so that I could write in peace; to former students at Cal State Bakersfield who read and criticized the first draft of the manuscript; to the good people of Spring Hill College who let me use the facilities there while I was on leave from Cal State; to my parents, Sam and Lillian Betty of Mobile, for their helpful criticisms and financial support; and to my father-in-law, Robert Doyle of Mobile, for letting me and my family hole up in his summer cottage on Mobile Bay, where, on a cool moonlit night in the spring of 1985, I last heard the whippoorwill sing.

Stafford Betty